Contents

Some words are shown in bold, **like this**. You can find out what they mean by looking in the glossary.

What is a car?

A car is part of everyday life in many places.

A car is a machine that moves along on wheels. Many people use cars to go to school or work every day. Inside a car there are seats for the driver and the passengers.

Transport

r

s

le

Please return/renew this item
by the last date shown.
Books may also be renewed by
phone and Internet

Heinemann
LIBRARY

BROMLEY LIBRARIES

3 0128 70093 7637

www.heinemann.co.uk
Visit our website to find out more information about Heinemann Library books.

To order:
 Phone 44 (0) 1865 888066
 Send a fax to 44 (0) 1865 314091
 Visit the Heinemann Bookshop at www.heinemann.co.uk to browse our catalogue and order online.

First published in Great Britain by Heinemann Library,
Halley Court, Jordan Hill, Oxford OX2 8EJ, part of Pearson Education.
Heinemann is a registered trademark of Pearson Education Ltd.

© Pearson Education Ltd 2000, 2008
This edition first published in paperback in 2008
The moral right of the proprietor has been asserted.

Editorial: Diyan Leake and Kristen Truhlar
Design: Kimberley R. Miracle and Ray Hendren
Picture research: Erica Martin
Production: Julie Carter

Originated by Chroma Graphics (Overseas) Pte Ltd
Printed and bound in China by South China Printing Co. Ltd

ISBN 978 0 4310 8696 5 (hardback)
12 11 10 09 08
10 9 8 7 6 5 4 3 2 1

ISBN 978 0 4310 8706 1 (paperback)
12 11 10 09
10 9 8 7 6 5 4 3 2

British Library Cataloguing in Publication Data
Oxlade, Chris
Transport Around the World: Cars

A full catalogue record for this book is available from the British Library

Acknowledgements
The publishers would like to thank the following for permission to reproduce photographs: Alamy p. **4** (Duncan Snow); Allsport pp. **20** (Mark Thompson), **21** (David Taylor), **28** (David Taylor); Auto-express pp. **5** (Dave Smith), **16**, **27** (Dave Smith); Corbis pp. **8** (Bettmann), **12**, **13** (David G. Hauser), **14** (David G. Hauser), **15** (W. Perry Conway); Image Bank p. **19** (L.D. Gordon); Quadrant pp. **9** (Flight), **10** (Felix), **18** (Simon Matthews), **22** (Pete Trafford); The Stock Market pp. **11**, **17**; Tony Stone Images pp. **7** (Christopher Bissell), **21** (Paul Souders), **24** (Simon Bruty), **25** (David Madison); Trip pp. **6** (H. Rogers), **23** (D. Palais), **26** (H. Rogers).

Cover photograph of a Bugatti Veyron reproduced with permission of Rex Features (Paul Cooper).

The publishers would like to thank Carrie Reiling for her assistance in the publication of this book.

Every effort has been made to contact copyright holders of any material reproduced in this book. Any omissions will be rectified in subsequent printings if notice is given to the publishers.

steering wheel

pedals

Drivers need to know how to use all the controls in a car.

The car goes to the left or right when the driver turns the **steering wheel**. The driver makes the car go faster or slower by using pedals. The pedals are on the floor of the car.

How cars work

Most cars have four wheels. Each wheel has a **rubber** tyre. The tyres roll along the road and stop the car sliding sideways as it goes round a corner.

Tyres need to be changed when they get damaged.

The person who fixes a car is called a **mechanic**.

Every car has an **engine** which makes the wheels turn round. The engine needs **fuel** to make it work. The fuel is stored in a large **tank**.

Old cars

One of the first cars was made in 1885. It was built by Karl Benz of Germany. It was like a **carriage** but it had an **engine** instead of a horse to pull it along.

The first cars like this were very noisy and quite dangerous.

At first, very few people could afford a car. When the Model-T Ford was built, it was cheap enough for many people to buy. More than 15 million Model-T Fords were made.

This Model-T Ford had a top speed of 72 kilometres (45 miles) per hour.

Classic cars

Some cars are special because of the way they look. They are called classic cars. Classic cars are often old cars that have been looked after carefully.

This classic Ford Thunderbird was built in the United States in 1956.

Some people collect classic cars. They spend hours polishing all the parts of the car. They display the car at classic car shows.

Many classic cars have shiny trim and fancy lights.

Where cars are used

These cars are travelling in a big city.

Most cars travel along roads. Roads are hard and smooth. Lines are painted on roads to show drivers the lanes they should drive in.

Cars that drive on dirt tracks
are heavy and strong.

In some places there are no proper roads so cars travel on dirt tracks. The tracks are often rough and bumpy. In the winter they can become very muddy.

Four-wheel drive

In a four-wheel-drive car the **engine** is joined to all four wheels. This makes it easier to drive the car along muddy or icy roads. Four-wheel-drive cars can go up very steep hills.

tyre

Cars with four-wheel drive have wide tyres.

tread

Tread stops the wheels from slipping in mud or ice.

Four-wheel-drive cars have tyres with a chunky **rubber** pattern, called tread. They have big wheels. The wheels keep the bottom of the car high off the bumpy ground.

Family cars

SUV is short for *sport utility vehicle*. SUVs often have more seats than other family cars. Big SUVs can be driven on rough, muddy, or icy roads.

SUVs are used in cities as well as in the country.

There is plenty of room for people and shopping in a big family car.

Many family cars need to have a lot of space. Family cars need to have a big boot. Sometimes the seats in cars fold down to make space for shopping or holiday luggage.

Limousines

A limousine is a very long, smart car. The person who drives it is called a chauffeur. People hire limousines for special occasions.

A limousine driving down the street always attracts attention.

The seats inside a limousine are big and comfy, like armchairs. Some limousines have a television and a telephone. Some even have a fridge for drinks.

television

A limousine has plenty of space to have meetings or to relax.

Stock cars

In Britain, stock cars are family cars used for racing around oval **tarmac** tracks. They are allowed to bump and bash into each other. Strong bars protect the driver in case the car rolls over.

Stock cars are made strong so that the driver does not get hurt.

In the United States,
stock cars go very fast.

Stock car racing is very popular in parts of the
United States. The cars race but they are not allowed
to bump into each other. The drivers get in the car
through a window instead of using the door.

Dragsters

tyres

Dragsters have a shape that helps them go very fast.

Dragsters are racing cars that race along a short, straight track. They have huge **engines**. Dragsters have monster tyres covered with sticky **rubber**.

parachutes

helmet

Dragster drivers wear helmets
to keep them safe.

A drag race only lasts for a few seconds, but the
cars can reach 320 kilometres (200 miles) per hour.
The cars slow down using parachutes at the end of
the race.

Racing cars

Car racing takes place on a special track. The cars travel at up to 350 kilometres (220 miles) per hour. It takes a lot of skill to drive a racing car.

Car racing is very exciting to watch.

wing

Mechanics work quickly so that a pit stop takes only a few seconds.

As the car speeds along, air goes over and under its wing. The air presses the car down so that it does not slide about on the corners. The car makes a **pit stop** when it needs work on it.

Electric and hybrid cars

Some cars have an **electric motor** instead of an **engine.** Batteries inside the cars make the electricity that the motor needs. The batteries need to be recharged when the electricity is used up.

This electric car is small and does not use too much **fuel**. It is just right for city driving.

A hybrid car uses less fuel than a normal petrol-fueled car.

A hybrid car uses both petrol and electricity. It can go as fast and as far as normal petrol-fueled cars. It does not cause as much **pollution** as other cars.

Jet power

A car called Thrust SSC was built to go faster than the speed of sound. It can travel faster than 1,250 kilometres (775 miles) per hour. This is as fast as a fighter aircraft can fly.

Thrust SSC was made to go faster than any other vehicle on land.

Thrust SSC has **engines** taken from a jet aircraft. A jet of hot gases shoots out of the back of the engines. This pushes the car forwards.

Timeline

1885 The first proper car is built in Germany by Karl Benz. It has three wheels and is driven along by a petrol **engine**. Its top speed is 13 kilometres (8 miles) per hour.

1894 The first proper motor race starts in Paris, France. The cars race each other to the city of Rouen.

1906 The first luxury Rolls-Royce car is sold. It is built by British engineers Charles Rolls and Henry Royce.

1908 In the United States, the Ford Motor Company builds the first Model-T Ford. The company is started by Henry Ford.

1936 The first Volkswagen Beetle is built in Germany.

1996 General Motors builds the first modern electric car that people can buy.

1997 Toyota builds the first hybrid car that people can buy. The Toyota Prius is first sold in Japan but becomes very popular in the United States by 2003.

2004 BMW unveils the world's fastest car powered by hydrogen gas. It is called the H2R and can go faster than 300 kilometres (185 miles) per hour.

Glossary

battery   a store of electricity. The electricity is gradually used up as the battery is used.

carriage   wheeled vehicle usually pulled by a horse

electric motor   a machine that powers movement using electricity. Electric cars have an electric motor.

engine   a machine that powers movement using fuel. A car's engine moves the car along.

fuel   anything that burns to make heat. In a car the fuel is a liquid called petrol or diesel oil.

mechanic   person who fixes cars

pit stop   when a racing car stops during a race to get new tyres and more fuel

pollution   waste and poisons that go into the air, water, and soil

rubber   a soft substance used to make tyres for vehicles

steering wheel   wheel inside a car that makes it go left or right

tank   container in a car where fuel is stored

tarmac   mixture of small stones and sticky tar which makes up the smooth surface of a road

Find Out More

Getting Around by Car, Cassie Mayer (Heinemann Library, 2006).

I Like Cars, Angela Aylmore (Heinemann Library, 2007).

Machines at Work: Cars and Bikes, Ian Graham (QED, 2007).

Wheels, Wings and Water: Cars, Chris Oxlade (Raintree, 2004).

World's Greatest Racing Cars, Ian Graham (Raintree, 2005).

Index